SKETCH
Book

This book belongs to:

____